CW01638413

Superposition

Superposition

Lauren O'Donovan

SOUTHWORD*editions*

First published in 2025
by Southword Editions
The Munster Literature Centre
Frank O'Connor House, 84 Douglas Street
Cork, Ireland

Set in Adobe Caslon 11pt

ISBN 978-1-915573-20-9

the arts council an chomhairle ealaíon
funding literature

Contents

Superposition /ˌs(j)uː.pə(ɹ).pəˈzɪʃ.ən/ *noun*

1. In quantum mechanics, superposition describes a state where multiple possibilities exist at once — until observed, until measured, until the future arrives and uncertainty collapses into certainty.
2. Superposition is the principle by which multiple elements exist simultaneously, layered without merging. In geology, older rock formations lie beneath newer ones. In music, harmonies stack, distinct yet interwoven. In cognition, thoughts, memories, and perceptions overlap, shaping experience.

For my husband, Steve
and the small girl, Rosie

October

Just like that, the set changes:
a tunnel of trees stretching the length of our road,
canopy blazing orange — the colour of death for leaves.

Hopping toward the bird feeder, I dodge pools of dissolved dog litter.
Starlings and sparrows glare at me from distant branches,
waiting for suet balls as they wait for the blackberry

to blister up from small white flowers; as they wait for spring eggs,
knowing — and yet, how can anyone know — what will come after
a crack and the arrival of another wet, hungry beak.

I watch a video where a fledgling magpie holds open its mouth,
aimed at a caterpillar, expecting the fat insect to jump inside,
confused by diligent parents tending to everything.

A greenfinch lands in the back garden —
quick as a kickboxer, she whips a foot to a dandelion's neck,
pins it down, stabs the wish flower with her beak.

One o'clock, two o'clock…
The small girl brings home a paper ghost with tissue trails
and wonders if his face is too sweet, his tongue too cheeky.

I hesitate for weeks, delaying the first press of the heating switch,
worried the oil was stolen while summer wasn't looking.
Swallows fly overhead in shifting alphabets.

November

Skeleton arms, forgotten since Halloween, reach up
from the front garden — still grasping for the legs of children.
The small girl swaps her rain jacket for a navy winter coat

stuffed with feathers plucked from eight-week-old geese.
The fake fur trim frames her face like the plastic icicles
twinkling round the windows of our neighbour's house.

The wipers swipe away melting ice with two easy swishes
and suddenly I'm belted in the backseat of my mother's car
with my brother, eating school-run cereal from a cup

as my mother pours warm water on the frozen windscreen.
A crack snaps — now lightning trapped in glass.
My brother drops his cup.

The collective noun for rotten leaves could be: a slip, a fall.
They're murder. In commercial egg production, they trick
the hens to think it's spring all year with artificial light.

Grey mould creeps along the bottom of an abstract painting
hung in the hall — I don't think to grab the vinegar
until the small girl thumbs the fuzz.

The battery in the digital display declaring *Pregnant*
lasts longer than the pregnancy. I order pizza
soaked with red sauce, clotted with congealed cheese.

Dear Small Girl

This morning, I was a robin in the garden, hiding
under the bent blades of a daffodil, and you
were a blueberry in the grass. You screamed
with laughter when I caught you,
pecking off little bites, filling myself up.

In my mind, I rehearse our future conversations,
while you're at school, while you sleep — cocooned
in monster-proof sheets, snoring like a puppy —
while you swing with a foot-push, then a bent-knee pull,
between girlhood and what's next.

I wish I could slow life down — let us stop
and hold this moment
in the cupped bowl of your determined hands

like that day at Iona Beach
when you held those stunned songbirds,
caught in cloth bags, weighed, and banded,
then placed in your waiting palms until you were ready
to blow on their feathered bellies like birthday candles.

December

Frozen mushrooms bloom like galaxies in the grass
at the Christmas tree farm. Workers chopped
the tops off orphans grown too tall to find a home;

now they stand like supermarket bonsais with branches
curved in like hands in prayer, each racing the other
to become the new trunk before they're lumber.

I bring the small girl shopping in town and spend
the whole day saying no. Storm winds toss
cigarette butts around the garden, whipped

from my hiding spot behind the silver-leaved
potted plant, a gift from my mother — I neglect it,
but it refuses to do anything but thrive.

The tremor in a friend's hand tells me how much
he's been drinking. I look away, see an unsteady pigeon
pecking at vomit, drunk on pickled chunks of last night.

The small girl invites me to her salon,
does my hair, nails, make-up — Raggedy Ann cheeks,
bright blue eyeshadow. She keeps telling me

how beautiful I am. I delete the pregnancy app, aborting
the baby growing in one sudden leap each week —
only her zeros remain to haunt the cloud.

January

I spread my alarms like hot butter
and they melt all over the bed. Anovulation
/ ˌænɒvjʊˈleɪʃən / *noun*, failure to produce eggs

or to discharge them from an ovary.
I am a bad chicken —
can't even lay once a month.

My mother texts, excited she saw a goldcrest
plucking strands of spiderweb to weave a softer nest.
How sweet, she says, with no thought for the spider.

Hand smudges on the mirror like faces of lost souls
shrieking at me from inside their prison; I exorcise
them with Windex and wish all hauntings went so easy.

The small girl throws another tantrum and I want
to slap her — to force her to submit. Instead I take a breath,
count to ten, wonder why I want to do all this again.

Two robins hop on my porch, looking like they rang the bell
and now wait to come in. A blackbird with a bright orange beak
swoops down, startles the robins.

It locks one bulging eye to mine, shits a splat of white.
If birds are messengers of the dead, then what missive
has some ghost just delivered to my front door?

In Japanese fairy tales, infertile couples find magical children

My fingers bleed from breaking bamboo

I max my credit card buying
all the melons in the supermarket
carve careful windows in their rind

Pull apart a thousand ripe, river-borne peaches
I don't know what to do
with all this rotting flesh

I visit every place said to hold a god
leave prayers and promises
my love without height conditions

Catch a family of sparrows
make a cut on each small pink tongue
they give me only silence

I kill the dog I love and burn him
rub his ashes into bark
make a dead tree blossom

And yet,
and yet —

February

Every time I see a daffodil, I'm struck how they all look the same —
brazen yellow cups, loitering on the green, smoking cigarettes,
bullying the heirlooms for their homemade skirts

and off-brand blooms. I have an elaborate dream
where I survive the years post-apocalypse
but can't find any decent socks. A pair of swans ignore

the porridge tossed by the small girl, now clotting in the pond,
instead nibble-slap their beaks at moss edges, looking
for answers — or insects. I wonder, under the water,

do they clasp each other's webbed feet?
A wild toddler flings duck feed at a mallard arranging her nest
while overhead, careless gulls surf the spring wind.

Sometimes the injections don't hurt at all, puncturing clean
the pinched mountain of fat at my waist, quietly depositing
fridge-cold hormones. Other times, the thin needle,

sharp as a memory, pierces a blood vessel
and leaves it bleeding beneath my skin, only a single drop
as proof until spectacular shades of indigo and umber

swirl into a bruise between my ovary and womb.
A cloud in the shape of a giant letter Y shouts across the wet sky,
and I think to myself, *Good question.*

March

The rose canes, thorn-thick and feared dead,
have sprouted sudden garlands of fresh leaves —
deep emerald, baby-bright, perfect now

before the wet, black-spot summer, before
the sawfly and aphids, before the rust,
the scale, the gall — the blindness of the blooms.

The small girl sobs because she will go to sleep six
and wake up seven, unable to prevent the transformation
she once looked forward to. She can't stop it,

no more than the caterpillar can stop the cocoon.
Another ultrasound of an empty womb, another
sharps bin emptied, another prescription bag in the fridge.

I start taking photographs of empty things:
a mayonnaise-smeared, crumpled cardboard sandwich box;
a roofless, burned-out house; a plastic milk carton washed up

on the sand; a bird's nest tumbling in the waves — spinning,
sinking, surfacing again — suspended between ebb and flood.
What happened to the eggs?

Male parts of alder trees litter the footpath
with long, bulbous catkin ropes. We crush them underfoot,
inhale their seed, grow saplings in our lungs.

Mono No Aware

Cherry blossom trees, too, are terrible
at sowing seeds, yet they make a grand show
of this failure — flinging into bloom
like debutantes, dizzy with their own arrival,

only to collapse, drunk on excess,
shoes lost, dresses torn, sinking
into slick mush, rotting into concrete,
drenching April in pink and white sex.

Still, as they empty themselves,
they are beautiful. They are spring
spilling over paths, blanketing city streets,
riding the wind in quiet storms of twirling silk.

I hide my petals in my underwear,
bury them by the toilet brush in a dusty metal bin.

Mono no aware (物の哀れ, "*the pathos of things*"): A Japanese term for the bittersweet awareness of impermanence.

April

Upon learning of the stone rolled back from the tomb,
the small girl declares she no longer likes Easter
because she's afraid of zombies. I remind her,

in our house, we celebrate life, and to never
make direct eye contact with an undead god.
After the first grass cut of the year, starlings peck

and step around the garden, their shivering wings
an iridescent spectrum of irreverent colours.
Early daffodil trumpets have withered, limp and brown,

incubating impossible seeds. What is the point
of all those loud flowers when bulbs reproduce
in the wet, dark, starless soil? The ultrasound screen

sloshes with circles of black, a void that means
presence, not absence — a sweet, fat egg, but
on the wrong side. That fallopian tube

became a coffin for a coffee-bean-sized baby.
Another month, another cancellation. More hormones
mean I'll be heavy with void eggs — a rare, featherless

chicken laying vantablack omelettes. The universe
may not be locally real, but my reality is local.
A fun-fair sign informs me: *Crying is not an emergency.*

May

The beech trees this year scream abundance,
branch after branch bushing out from bottom trunks —
soil to sky, an infinity of heart-shaped wings.

That woman pushing a baby in a buggy — can she feel
the weight of my ambition in her tired arms?
Tiny globes of dandelion seed bob in the grass,

waiting for the tipping point: a sharp breeze, a child's kick —
perched at the precise moment between their peak
and a sudden death / burst of new life.

The small girl asks a fly what it prefers: a flick or a blow.
On the park wall, two crows sway like stoned surfers,
staring up at Basant festival kites:

thin coloured paper stretched on stick skeletons,
trailing long plumes of crepe ribbons —
squint hard enough, they might be hawks.

It's embarrassingly easy to propagate a pothos;
should I cut off my baby finger, leave it to root
in a glass jar on the windowsill?

The fates weave DNA, not cloth, the genetic
testing nurse states. If each child were a coin,
the chance of three-in-a-row is one-in-eight.

Superposition

I book tickets for a concert
next year existing in multiple realities
simultaneous until realised

In one
          we can't go because we have a newborn

In another
          we will never have another child

June

Hens can store a rooster's sperm for weeks, fertilise
one egg a day, then incubate a whole clutch to hatch at once.
Summer ditches bruise foxglove purple and gorse yellow.

A newly fledged starling is stuck in the cylindrical body
of the wire bird feeder — struggling, twisting —
its ambivalent brothers pecking at the suet balls below.

When I get close enough to attempt rescue,
I see panic in one bright eye — the bird whirls into a blur
of feather, erupts from the feeder's broken mouth unharmed.

When you wish upon a star, they say you're already too late.
A walking sunbeam — the dog pads indoors
carrying a gift of hot cosmos trapped in his fur.

At my father's grave, I give the small girl spare roses.
She places them in one of the empty pots by a memorial photo
of a smiling woman, says: *Maybe whoever used to bring her flowers died too.*

Collared doves scavenge in the garden — I could
rush out with a towel, catch one, maybe two — keep them
as pets, convert the shed into an aviary, bring the sky home.

How a dead thing is unmistakable
from a sleeping thing, like life itself is visible —
the body just crumpled fabric of flesh and feather.

July

My brother reads wishes tied to a hawthorn tree
in Kenmare town — hundreds of folded white papers
that flutter as if trying to lift the short tree higher.

The clouds look like they've been rolled out
by a badly floured pin; some god is baking biscuits.
At the butterfly conservatory, they keep the wings

of the dead to use as prosthetics for the living.
The small girl buries a bumblebee, curled foetal,
missing legs, all the gloss lost from its fuzz.

She digs a grave in moss with a silver spoon —
a moment that still exists as a distant band of light
travelling forever through the endless expansion of space.

A woman talks about inheriting an African grey parrot
who says things in her late father's voice
like, *Yes dear*, and, *Time to play sudoku.*

My husband and I take a cabin on the ferry for an hour.
I find his blue eyes in the vanity mirror — my elbows bent
on the table, linen skirt rolled up around my waist.

In the Netherlands I would be called: *wish-mother.*
Under a microscope, tears dried to crystals look different
depending on what you felt when you cried.

Moss

I take toy shovelfuls of dirt
from the forest, different spots:
by the feet of tall wildflowers,
under an oak tree — its twisting
roots littered with acorns —
from the hard-packed path.

I plant it in a glass terrarium, water it. Wait.
Weeks pass, and nothing grows.
How can soil be so barren?

But then — one tiny strand of feather moss.
A single tendril rising
from the deep brown,
like a hand put up,
saying: *Me, I'm here.*
I live.

August

Can a hen grow a whole egg in just one day?
If you kick a chicken's abdomen, does the egg
crack, spilling yolk and whites inside?

The small girl tells me to stop talking about
simulation theory because it makes her sad
to wonder if our hugs are real.

For the first injection, I was a short-breath mess,
pricking myself again and again because I couldn't
push it all the way in. Now I'm a junkie,

each needle chasing motherhood — the letdown
of milk into the mewling mouth of a new king.
They ready me for surgery while my husband

ejaculates into a plastic cup. Then nine cells
float in the viscous universe of my uterus.
I curse us by giving the embryo a name —

the pregnancy tests insist on being as white
as I've always wanted my teeth to be.
In the multiverse, causality runs in reverse:

the present determines the past, not the other way
around — of infinite paths, the only one that persists
is the one that leads to where we currently are.

September

In Helsinki, a dandelion wish lands in my hair.
I try to free it, but it clings to the sweat on my fingers —
the parachute folds, fine hairs clump together

under the weight of my moisture. I flick it off
onto concrete, where it will die before it lives.
It's said butterflies can't see their own wings —

they can, they're just too focused ahead to look back.
It's someone's job to sort fluffy yellow chicks,
then kill the half that are male.

A wood pigeon's wings slap heavy as thunder
as it fights gravity, achieving an ungainly lurch
into air that manages to catch the lucky bird

just a second before the cat.
I snap off another chunk of Galaxy share bar —
it doesn't even last a minute on the lips.

Is it a sin to chew chocolate instead of savouring
the melted suck of every bite? If I relax my stomach,
lean slightly back, I am bigger than when I was ready

to give birth to the small girl. But now there's nothing
inside me except depleted ovaries, constipated bowels,
and one tired heart beating.

Acknowledgements & Notes

I am profoundly grateful to the Munster Literature Centre for its tireless work in sustaining a vibrant Irish literary culture, and for the invaluable opportunities it offers writers. It has been—and continues to be—an immeasurable joy for *Superposition* to win the Fool for Poetry Chapbook Competition, and to have this chapbook join the shelves alongside previous winners I so deeply admire.

With thanks to the editors of the following publications where poems from this chapbook first appeared: *Southword, Poetry Ireland Review, Banshee*, and *The Stony Thursday Book.* Special thanks to Cork City Libraries, Creative Ireland, and Poetry in the Park for selecting 'Dear Small Girl' for display in Cork parks.

The completion of this manuscript was made possible by the generous support of Cork County Council's Artists' Creative Bursary Scheme.

I am also immensely grateful for the guidance, feedback, and support of peers, mentors, and literary organisations, without whom I would be a much poorer poet. In particular, my thanks to Molly Twomey, James Harpur, Jessica Traynor, Róisín Leggett Bohan, Lucy Holme, Victoria Kennefick, Rosamund Taylor, Afric McGlinchey, Thomas McCarthy, Joanne McCarthy, D'or Seifer and the amazing Lime Square Poets, Mathew Geden and The Cork Poetry Collective, Paul Casey and everyone at Ó Bhéal, the English Department faculty and my classmates at University College Cork, Moze Jacobs and the team at DeBarra's Spoken Word, Annemarie Ní Churreáin and my cohort at The Stinging Fly Summer School, Paul Muldoon and the Finny Tribe Writing Group, the Patrick Kavanagh Centre and Patrick Kavanagh Society, and to all those I have connected with only briefly but who have left a lasting impact on my work.

To the pioneers of IVF, who battled stigma and bravely faced the unknown—thank you.

Finally, my wholehearted thanks to my wonderful family and friends for their patience, love, and relentless support. In particular, my love and thanks to Steve, Rosie, Logan, Leonne, Alan, Andrew, Maia, Julie, Carol, Janet, Mary, Catherine, Rachel, Shantel, Becky, Steven M., Gunnhilder, Justin, Sara, Shane, Pete, Angela, Steve H., Teresa, Elaine, and all the O'Donovans, Cavanaghs, Hogans, Kellehers, and Walshes.

'In Japanese fairy tales, infertile couples find magical children' is inspired by the following stories from Japanese folklore: *The Tale of the Bamboo Cutter, Uriko-hime (Melon Princess), Momotarō (Peach Boy), Tongue-Cut Sparrow, The Old Man Who Made Flowers Bloom,* and *Issun-bōshi (One-Inch Boy).*

Printed in Great Britain
by Amazon

61326624R00020